bent twigs & wet feet

a free verse book of poetry

by Elliot M. Rubin

Copyright April 2019
Library of Congress

ISBN13 - 978-0-9981796-8-1

ISBN10 - 0-9981796-8-X

No part of this book may be reproduced in any form whatsoever without the prior, express written consent of the author.

This book is fiction, and all names, people, places, and happenings are from the author's imagination and are used fictionally.

Any resemblance to any living or dead persons, and/or businesses, locations and/or events is coincidental in its entirety.

All rights reserved

Dedication

To my darling Laura

for bearing with me all these years.

Preface

Free verse poetry allows a story to be told without rhyming or a mathematical structure restricting the flow of words.

This collection tells varied stories, I hope you enjoy them.

Table of Contents

bent twigs and wet feet 7
erotic flesh 8
still in my life 9
i'm a Cadillac Girl 10
chocolate challah 12
first amendment 13
going home 14
understanding 16
a realization 18
miss you 19
my daughter 20
water 22
the bakery 23
a young brunette divorcé 24
the moment 26
the old Brooklyn Madam 28
the senior community center 30
urban princess 32
why? 33
winter storm 34
A sestina for Christina 36
in memory of Michael Seitz 38
oddity 39
broken glass 40
addiction 41
Spring flowers 42

forgetting	43
the dominatrix librarian	44
truth	45
merry-go-round	46
the used book store	48
strange conversation	50
Rivington and Clinton Streets	52
chains	53

bent twigs and wet feet

in the mountains of Vermont
high above a valley,
i walk along a path
with low undergrowth
small twigs crack
under my feet,
inhaling
crisp, clean
unpolluted air-
far from the city;
letting my mind wander
aimlessly
with not a care in the world

a narrow creek ahead
is flowing fast, ponding in a crook

as sun is at its height
during summer, the heat
melts my clothes
forcing me to visit
the cold fresh water
getting my feet wet first,
sitting to cool off
as the icy current
splashes
on my back,
repeating and repeating
in a soothing pattern,
moving me
into a meditation
of mindlessness

erotic flesh

his skin
taut
tan
shaved
smooth
chiseled muscles

her skin
soft
pliable
supple
no tan lines
on a curved body

flesh is organic,
wanting to be touched,
caressed,
held close with
stimulating neurons
electrifying the brain-
flushing hormones
through veins-
the mind
screams
in orgasmic ecstasy,
exhausting the body;
causing it
to relax

go limp

then sleep

still in my life

sometimes, they stay
talking and stirring
your mind,
forever in your life-
memories never leaving

some are youthful friends
or lusty past loves
still tugging
at your emotions;
roiling your life

decades fly by so fast-
the future is finite,
the past is now the present-
ghosts can live with you forever

i'm a Cadillac Girl

i'm a Cadillac girl
  in a Chevy world,
my tastes are fine
  like expensive wine,
real pearls i like
  but i'm out of luck.
the ones i wear
  are like Two Buck Chuck

i want to travel
  go near and far
my talent keeps me
  in this dive bar.
someday i'll make it
  out of here
drinking scotch
  and no more beer

it's good looking guys
  i really like.
but its beer belly men
  all named Mike,
with matted beards
  and smell like hell,
who want me now
  but dumb as well

they're out of work
   and don't do squat
i want the guys
   who know what's what,
who make some money
   a lot of dough,
don't make excuses
   like on furlough

i wait for Sunday
   to hear the bell
praise the Lord
   and give as well
i go to church
   and work really hard
singing in a
   sequined leotard

i play the lottery
   every week
just like working
   nine to five
nothing's changed
   i'm getting pooped
same old same old
   every year

i'm a Cadillac girl
   in a Chevy world,
old shoes are tight
   my toes are curled,
my ambition grand
   my wants unfurled,
i'm a Cadillac girl
   in a Chevy world

chocolate challah

the softness is sensual
  sweet to the taste,
    the braids are for gripping
      it's chocolate addictive

hand rolled and baked
  waiting to be savored,
    the chocolate embedded
      then melted in the dough

one bite will tell you
  two will convince,
    the third is orgasmic
      you can't eat enough

they call it chocolate challah
  it's manna from heaven,
    this bet you will win
      it's better than cake!

no butter is needed
  or grape jelly too,
    everyone will love it
      and definitely you!

first amendment

i don't like their writing
or the thoughts they endorse,
i try to be mainstream,
not extreme like they are

if the opinions or beliefs
some hold are silenced,
i know a boomerang
flies back to the thrower

i value free speech,
news and video;
though their tongues
may be silenced
for a while

don't swaddle their voice

loudly,
let us all speak out

going home

driving back
to my childhood home
for one last peek
at my long past youth,
memories rush in,
bringing themselves
into my consciousness,
becoming aware
of their presence-
mentally seeing my friends
where we played
touch football
in front of our homes,
sewer cover to sewer cover
the line of scrimmage
is a glob of white spit
on black asphalt,
as we threw and ran the ball
all over the street;
never
stepping on streaks
of saliva
going from one goal
to the next,
making end run plays
or catches,
trying not to walk
on the starting line
as we counted
three Mississippi seconds
to start a play

standing
in front of my parents
former home,
i see the boys
of long ago
 in my mind's eye;
sitting on the red brick stoop
talking
about subjects
of no importance today,
things I can't recall,
but were significant then

i vividly remember
teenage girls from school,
teenage girls we played with,
teenage girls we dated,
all gone…

dispersed into adulthood
like throwing seeds in the air,
carried away to mature elsewhere,
only to be imagined decades later
in my dreams and thoughts

understanding

help me understand God;
things happen which
make no sense to me
nor to many others,
if you believe there is a God

help me understand God;
so many genocides took place
in the history books i don't
have enough fingers and toes
to count them all

help me understand God;
though terrible evil happens
people still believe there
is a merciful God,
who looks out for all

help me understand God;
all soldiers in war will tell you
God is in every foxhole,
yet is always on both sides-
with youth dying in combat

help me understand God;
why young children die,
innocents all, some stricken
with the worst diseases
or deformities possible?

help me understand God;
we attribute goods things
occurring to a heavenly
guide, but we don't know
why wickedness should exist

help me understand God;
we have free choice, yet
everything is preordained.
is the belief a comfort to our
mind when the end comes?

help me understand God!

a realization

standing on slimy
slippery moss
deep in the woods,
by the low bank
of a shallow
country creek,
crystal clear currents
gently collide
against a rock
jutting above the water,
stuck in the mud,
small air bubbles
permeating ripples
as small fish
flash by the stone

at the last second
they veer around
rocks and wood in their path,
avoiding a collision
by the smallest space
 imaginable

caught in this cognitive moment,
i realize we are all like the fish

we go about our lives
as best we can,
trying to avoid disaster and harm
until we can't

trapped in the current of life

miss you

when dark clouds
  in life
    bring me down

thinking of you
  makes the sun
    shine through

i can write
  a love poem
    even with
      a broken heart

my daughter

she was beautiful,
just beautiful;
her smile
went from cheek to cheek,
always a good word
for everyone

Harvard,
Princeton,
Yale,
they all wanted her
to attend,
her intelligence
shone bright
attracting the world's
greatest minds

coming from a family
who valued
compassion,
kindness,
learning-
there was nothing
she could not accomplish
once she set her mind
to the task

i totally,
massively,
and with every ounce
of my being
mourn her loss;
my girl
never had a chance-
forty years ago
she died in utero
in her first trimester

water

when the warm August sky
turns to gray,
and tiny droplets fall from the sky,
we open umbrellas
waiting for the torrent
to pour down on us,
while we hide
from the downpour
not wanting to get wet;
as we inhale the sweet smell
of a summer rainstorm

yet at home
we turn our shower on
till it is a torrent,
standing under it for a long time
letting it soak all over our bodies,
closing our eyes tightly
while the water goes where it wants,
and the sweet smell of soap
penetrates our senses,
lulling us
into a passive trance

the bakery

the attractive display
in the window made me
stop, and look in the store
at the pastries under glass

the sugary swirls
on the sides of the cakes
brought my eyes up,
staring at the lone red cherry
with the long stem on top,
immersed in swirled whip cream
on a bed of chocolate waves

walking inside,
a buxom young woman
behind the counter
greeted me
see anything you would like?

i liked her muffins,
but decided
i should not say
what i am thinking

i don't know her well enough yet
to ask for them in that manner;
but there is always the next tray
to bring out and see what's on it

after all, a bakery
is all about good taste

a young brunette divorcé

she lived in the house
on the corner, a
pre-war brick building

a walk-up
with marble steps
on a steel encased stairway.

a darkened entry hall
feel like doom as you enter
behind frosted art deco
steel and glass front doors,

in the afternoons
she sat
on a beach chair
on the sidewalk
with other divorced women,
talking,
complaining,
comparing dates
or lack of them;
always looking
at men walking past

smiling at them,
encouraging
conversation,
while her sons played
behind her
with the other children
in front
of the building
behind

a chain link

often, she offered
a cold drink
on a hot day
to a passing young man

sometimes
they would go upstairs
the remaining women
sitting
in their beach chairs
watched the kids
for an hour or so

afterward,
she often had money
to buy dinner for her boys

the moment

i am…
the single red rose in a bushel of yellow,
the black dot on a white page,
a diamond surrounded by red rubies

i see…
humor where others don't,
a story in an incident i witness,
creative fiction in reality

as a young boy…
i daydreamed in elementary school,
i enjoyed listening to blues and jazz,
i purchased my first record -
Little Richard's Good Golly Miss Molly

looking back i am aware
of when the signs stood out,
but i did not understand them
at the time-

i was fourteen
growing up in a
stodgy,
conservative
middle-class area

walking past a shoe store
i spotted a pair of red,
patent leather shoes
in the window,
and wanted them
against
my mother's protestations;
but they didn't have my size

that was the moment
i realized
i was a unique individual

the backward fork in the drawer,
about to march to the beat
of my own making
in life

the old Brooklyn Madam
(around the corner)

the retiring grocer
told me about her;
she would barter
for his groceries

i remember seeing her

she was short,
maybe five feet tall,
rail thin,
tousled hair,
emaciated looking

always wearing
pointed torpedo shaped
brassieres,
heavy
pancake makeup,
thick red lipstick
plus stiletto heels
when she went out
before noon

never smiling
to anyone
she passed
on the street,
even if you smiled
or waved hello

she was a stern
looking woman;
but a typical Madam
one would find
in a house
of ill repute

surprisingly,
he told me
she had a solid business
of lust

i took his word for it

the senior community center

sitting in the grand ballroom
before the free movie starts
i look around,
the room is full
of old people,
barely walking,
a sea of pink
and blue hair
on women
who years ago
i would have found
to be exciting,
vibrant,
probably sexy;
now wrinkled,
doubled over,
with calcium deprived bones
holding on to canes
and chrome plated walkers

my mind wanders,
and i wonder
what their younger lives
might have been;
how many
weddings,
divorces
or affairs
they might have had

how many lovers
before marriage?
how many children,
before old age set in?

the truth is…

i'm sitting
in the room with them,
where i too belong

maybe they are thinking
the same thing
about me
before the movie begins?

or worse…

you never know

urban princess

holding the hands of
two young children
while waiting in line,
the welfare office
is a jumble of bodies
wandering aimlessly
behind a screened counter,
looking busy,
yet the line
doesn't move

two visiting princes
promised her castles;
they were hit
and run royalty,
leaving
two new jewels
in their crown;
down for hours,
gone for years

the landlord wants her out,
section eight wants her in,
the twelve-month wait
places a princess on the street

her priests ban abortions,
her politicians banned them too,
her life is in ruins,
where are they now?

who's to help?

why?

they are born in this country,
raised here,
went to school here,
English is the mother tongue

they wish to serve and protect
to the best of their abilities,
including the ultimate sacrifice

they have all the human frailties
a person can have;
love,
desire,
empathy,
ambition,
humor,
plus…
the ability to work hard,
vote, pay taxes

they are like everyone else
who want to serve
their country

but they are not allowed
to join armed services;
even if mentally
and physically able
because of a private
sexual gender preference

so i ask…

why?

winter storm

a blanket of white
covers the ground
leaving small
traceable footprints
where deer walked,
looking for something
to satisfy
their winter hunger

under a small pine tree
i see a red fox
curled up
trying to sleep,
its nose buried
deep in its fur
to keep warm

the rapid running
of squirrels is missing,
staying in their burrows
not venturing out
in the deep snow,
trying to avoid
the circling
hawks high above
looking
for a target
to stand out
against the purity
of the virgin snow,
and stain it red
with blood

inside
my warm home
i am drinking hot chocolate
while looking out
the window
at nature;
wondering
how those less fortunate
than i
are coping
in a country of plenty,
where empathy
is only found
in sermons

A sestina for Christina

I really don't want to write a sestina.
I'd rather be sleeping with Christina,
Or slurping a delicious pastina,
Maybe even dancing a Macarena.
While others seek words in a dictionary
I'd be listening to her sing like a canary.

Her skin color is similar to the canary
It varies almost like a sestina,
I am bored looking in a dictionary
While I could be with my Christina
Dancing around to the Macarena
While others will be eating pastina

Whether its Italian or Turkish pastina
Its yellow color looks like a canary
While people are dancing a Macarena
I really don't want to write a sestina
I'd rather be sleeping with Christina
Than looking up words in a dictionary

While others seek words in a dictionary
Or slurping a delicious pastina
I'd rather be sleeping with Christina
Or listen to her sing like a canary
But I need to finish this sestina
Before I can dance the Macarena

Maybe we all can dance the Macarena
while looking up words in a dictionary
Let others write a sestina
and cooking or slurping pastina,
But she does sing like a canary
While I'll be sleeping with Christina

I'd rather be sleeping with Christina
Or even dancing to a Macarena
And listen to her sing like a canary
While others seek words in a dictionary
Or slurping a delicious pastina
I really don't want to write a sestina

After Christina, I'll write a sestina
Before the Macarena or pastina,
Or the canary sings like a dictionary

in memory of Michael

he was an avid
hockey fan
always watching
his favorite team play,
though his body
was racked with pain

the disease sent him
to renown hospitals
for brain surgeries
and treatments,
but they did not help

always smiling
with good cheer
the end came
quietly,
swiftly,
sitting
in his favorite chair

too young
a man to go
he will be missed;
by all
who knew his
kindness and smile,
and those who never
had the luck
to meet him

oddity

they thought
i was odd

the truth being,
they are different

not i!

broken glass

sitting on the edge
of the foyer table,
located between
candlesticks and a
framed picture of her,
the glass vase
seemed secure

until she threw a fit
slamming
the heavy door
on her way out

shaking the table
sending everything
crashing
to the floor

splintering glass
into a thousand
broken pieces

like my heart

addiction

it flows
though my veins,
surging
into my mind
giving me
a sweet high
i can't resist

once i start
i can't stop

a few times a day
i must have it,
the pull
is irresistible

it is
my mistress,
my muse,
my compulsion,
my habit

oh, how i regret
ever staring with it.

stay away,
stay away,
from
irresistible
chocolate

Spring flowers

i remember her
as a newlywed
leaving the house,
walking to the
farmers field
to pick wildflowers;
placing them
in a clear glass vase
filled with water
on the kitchen table
when she returned

the spring colors
of light blue with
pale yellow petals,
surrounded
by lavender florets
and green leaves
brightened the start
of every new day

the farm is gone,
overgrown
like weeds
with new homes
decades later,

she too has passed
into memory

leaving me with
an empty vase

like my life is now

forgetting

i wanted to write
about forgetting,
but my thoughts
fled from my mind

the dominatrix librarian

dressed in all black
with five-inch stiletto heels,
she stands behind the desk
checking out books, and
the men in front of her

i always wondered
if she ever directed
them to the erotic
bookshelves section?

might she
suggestively quote
the Dewey decimal
system to them?

did she hope
they would withdraw
an arousing novel
from amongst
the tight,
leather
bound editions
she found
so stimulating?

the librarian
is the mistress
of the books,
keeping control
and order over
all she dominates

truth

a writer
has to write the truth,
no matter how hard,
or if it hurts others
as well as themselves,
because truth matters

the Queen of England
goes through the motions
to satisfy
politicians and public,
while she'd rather
ride in the fields
or cleaning her stables
with a shovel

the heroin addict
prostituting herself
at night to get a fix
regrets ever starting,
but has no way out
without help,
that is her truth

given facts,
real facts,
provable facts,
it is a writer's obligation
to let the sun shine
on the facts
come what may;
or truth
is not truth…
anymore

merry-go-round

watching the gaily
painted horses
going up and down
on the merry-go-round,
with small children
holding on
to the gold colored posts
while leather belts
are securely tightened
around their waists,
brings back memories
of when i was a child

i remember
my father standing
next to me,
holding onto my back,
just in case
i fell off
the hand painted
stallions,
as they rose and fell
while the loud
music blasted
in my ears

thinking about it
i realize life
is a merry-go-round
with ups and downs,
occasionally
falling off not using
care and foresight

sometimes,
you just can't
get back on
when you want

the used book store

if you stand
in a tire store
the smell
of the rubber
permeates your brain,
giving you
a semi-high feeling
of euphoria

a used bookstore
sometimes
has a similar
smell,
one of knowledge
emanating from the
old tattered pages of
books stacked
on bending shelves,
under the weight
sitting on top

reaching for one
which caught my eye
i opened it.
it is a book
about a young family,
a sad book,
there are small
tear stains
on the margins
tugging
at my heart

on the inside
back cover
it seems like
a woman's handwriting,
she wrote a short note
saying the book is about
her parents;
please say a prayer
for them
when you finish
reading their story

closing the book
i purchased it

bringing it
to my apartment
to sit
on my bookshelf,
joining my family,
giving it a home again

strange conversation

i noticed him
standing
on the corner
in Manhattan,
wearing
ill-fitting old clothes,
speaking to the air

people ignore him.

maybe they knew
better than i,
but i needed
to cross the street
at the corner,
that particular corner

the closer i came
the better i could
hear him stammer
to himself
something
about the president

i have to save the president
he kept repeating
to no one in particular

unfortunately
this is Manhattan;
no one seems to care
about him,
or what he's saying

when the light changed
i crossed the street;
others followed me
also ignoring him

the truth is
this is not unusual;
there are thousands more
like him
walking sidewalks
in an overcrowded city
in need of mental help,
never receiving it

Rivington and Clinton Streets

you can see the ghosts
of past immigrants
leaning out the windows,
hordes of people
negotiating sidewalks
with pushcart vendors
parked near the curb,
selling their wares
in an alien language-
families packed into
tenements, parents
raising families
in overcrowded
environments-
stifling in summer
freezing in winter;
working long hours
to make ends meet;
at the mercy of employers
abusing them
in hours and wages-
they believed in
the American dream;
freedom to worship,
ability to get ahead,
giving their children
a better life
than in the old country-
if you stand on that corner
and close your eyes
you might be able to hear them
still, their souls still floating about

chains

born into poverty,
she hustled
in her early life,
struggling in school,
seeing her self-worth
through a prism
of welfare
and food stamps

a high school teacher
took a liking
to her personality,
helped her
with her studies
so she graduated;
then went to a
free college

after graduating
she went to work;
throwing off
the mental chains
of impoverishment
and obtaining
the American dream
of personal success

a free education
was the difference

Other books by Elliot M. Rubin

A trilogy of 5 STAR action/adventure novels
    Hot Cash/Cold Bodies
    Kara Bennet - Vengeance
    Dead Girls Don't Die

Romance and Murder in Bensonhurst

Flash Fiction
    People Stories in 600 Words
    (as told by a raconteur)

Poetry
    Scrambled Poems from My Heart
    A Boutique Bouquet of Poems and Stories
    Rumblings of an Old Man
    Surf Avenue Girl and other poems

Jewish Satire
    The Phartick Chronicles

www.CreativeFiction.net

www.ingramcontent.com/pod-product-compliance
Lightning Source LLC
Chambersburg PA
CBHW051718040426
42446CB00008B/941